THE HAPPINESS
OF GOD

were reminiscent of ... and home Marie suddenly suggested to ... their Princess, that Therese, who had ... taken part in the conversation ...

THE HAPPINESS
OF GOD

Holiness in Thérèse of Lisieux

SUSAN LESLIE

ALBA · HOUSE   NEW · YORK

SOCIETY OF ST. PAUL, 2187 VICTORY BLVD., STATEN ISLAND, NEW YORK 10314

Library of Congress Cataloging-in-Publication Data

Leslie, Susan
    The happiness of God: holiness in Thérèse of Lisieux / by Susan Leslie.
        p.   cm.
    Bibliography: p.
    ISBN 0-8189-0540-9
    1. Thérèse, de Lisieux, Saint, 1873-1897.   2. Holiness — History of
doctrine — 19th century.   I. Title.
    BX4700.T5L43   1988
    282'.092'4 — dc19
    [B]   88-21658
                                              CIP

Designed, printed and bound in the United States of
America by the Fathers and Brothers of the
Society of St. Paul, 2187 Victory Boulevard,
Staten Island, New York 10314, as part of their
communications apostolate.

Printing Information:

Current Printing - first digit   3 4 5 6 7 8 9 10 11 12 13 14 15 16

Year of Current Printing - first year shown

                                                      1997   1998   1999

Contents

Preface

THERE ARE many books already in print on Thérèse of Lisieux, the young French Carmelite nun who died in 1897, aged 24. So why publish yet another book on her? First of all, this adolescent Carmelite and her writings are very modern and hold a spiritual message from which we all can draw inspiration even today. She represents for us the *actualité* of the Gospel. In the words of John Paul II "of Thérèse of Lisieux one can say with conviction that the spirit of God let her heart reveal directly to the men and women of our day the fundamental reality of the Gospel." The saint thus becomes an inexhaustible and untiring source of life and inspiration as the Gospel itself.

Again, we believe that the last word about holiness has not yet been said, especially when holiness coincides with the "happiness of God" and is the reflection of his unlimited love for man. Thérèse, who passionately longed to be a "priest, martyr and apostle" to save everyone,

teaches us that to become a saint, i.e., to be happy, is within the reach of every woman and man. The young, the oppressed, the sick, the poor, whose number is so great today and who feel powerless, useless and so small in a world governed by sheer composition and size, haunted by a sense of futility and frustration, can still be saints. For all the "little people," Thérèse of Lisieux, though she qualifies herself as "the little grain of sand," blazes a path of hope towards a meaningful life.

Cardinal Pacelli, at the time the Basilica in Lisieux was blessed, said of Thérèse: "The dazzling genius of Augustine, the luminous wisdom of Thomas Aquinas, have shed forth upon souls the rays of an imperishable splendor; through them, Christ and his doctrine have become better known. The divine poem lived out by Francis of Assisi has given to the world an imitation, as yet unequalled, of the life of God-made-man. Through him legions of men and women have learned to love God more perfectly. But a little Carmelite who had hardly reached adult age has conquered in less than half a century innumerable hosts of disciples. Doctors of the law have become children at her school; the Supreme shepherd has exalted her and prays to her with humble and assiduous supplications; and even at this moment from one end of the earth to the other, there are millions of souls

whose interior life has received the beneficient influence of the little book, 'The Autobiography.' "

Thérèse is like a magnet that attracts iron or the colors of the rainbow that captivates the attention of the young and old alike. This is why we publish this book: to share with you some of the happiness of God.

The Publisher

PART ONE

A SHORT LIFE

Introduction

THÉRÈSE MARTIN was born in 1873 in the Norman town of Alençon. She was the last of nine children of whom only five girls survived: Marie, Pauline, Léonie and Céline. Her parents, Louis Martin and Zélie Guérin, were devout Catholics. Although both had desired the religious life, both had been turned away by religious superiors. In marriage, they saw an opportunity to "raise saints for heaven." The Martin household was disciplined and cheerful. Religious fasts were rigorously observed, feasts and anniversaries celebrated with enthusiasm. Thérèse was the favorite child and enjoyed her position as baby of the family but she escaped being spoiled — only just, as her father doted on his 'Little Queen'; it fell to the mother and older sisters to keep Thérèse in line, which they did, firmly but kindly.

When Thérèse was four-and-a-half, Madame Martin died of breast cancer. Thérèse was deeply affected and was extremely easily given

to tears for years afterwards. Louis decided to move his girls to Lisieux so that they could benefit from the maternal oversight of his sister-in-law, Céline Guérin; her husband Isidore, Zélie's brother, a much more practical man than the somewhat dreamy Louis, was to become the guardian of the Martin girls.

Thérèse settled happily into her new home. She enjoyed romping with Céline in the garden, making little altars, teasing Papa to come and admire her handiwork. Marie and Pauline undertook Thérèse's early schooling. She was an intelligent pupil, gifted except in arithmetic and spelling; obstinate and inventive, she tried to persuade her teacher that French grammar was illogical and should cede to her own theories. 'Real' school, at the local Benedictine Abbey, was misery to Thérèse. She spent only five years there and completed her studies with a private tutor in the town.

At the age of nine, Thérèse overheard Marie and Pauline discussing Pauline's imminent entry into the local Carmelite monastery. The little girl was devastated. Pauline had been mother to her since Zélie's death; this was another 'death,' a very terrible separation for a rather nervous and highly sensitive child. Five months later, Thérèse succumbed to a violent attack of chorea, thought to have been precipitated by both her grief over Pauline and an ill-timed

conversation with Uncle Isidore about her dead mother. Thérèse became delirious and the family began to fear for her reason, then for her life. Masses were offered, desperate prayers made to the Blessed Virgin. During the most violent attack of all, Marie, Léonie and Céline knelt in prayer before a statue of Our Lady in Thérèse's bedroom. Thérèse, agonizingly lucid throughout the scene, joined her silent prayer to those of her sisters. Suddenly she saw the Virgin smiling at her and at once she knew she was cured. Marie, astonished at the sudden change in Thérèse, pried the story out of the reluctant invalid and then begged permission to tell the Carmelites. When Thérèse next visited the monastery, she was bombarded by eager questions. The nuns had expected to hear of a spectacular vision but little Thérèse could only repeat, "She was very beautiful and she *smiled* at me!", which understandably was thought to be an inadequate account. Thérèse began to wonder if the whole episode, illness and miraculous cure, had been play-acting on her part.

Thérèse's First Communion, a year later, coincided with Pauline's religious profession and was a day of double family rejoicing. Already Thérèse had decided that she, too, would become a Carmelite. She had even discussed the matter with the Prioress at the time of Pauline's entry but had been smilingly informed that one

did not enter a monastery at the age of nine; she set herself to wait. Marie became a Carmelite in 1886, thus depriving Thérèse of her second substitute mother. Meanwhile, Léonie had gone to join the Poor Clares. It was only natural that the two youngest, Céline and Thérèse, should also long to be nuns. However, it was not to be an "automatic" choice for either of them. There was to be much trial and testing before the two girls finally arrived at their goal. Thérèse, above all, was still very immature, weeping at the slightest provocation, demanding thanks and appreciation for the least good deed. It was at the end of this same year that Thérèse underwent her "complete conversion" which seems to have been a well-nigh miraculous leap into maturity. Freed at last from her tearfulness, she began to feel strong and not a little ambitious. She would be a saint! The following May, Thérèse begged her father's permission to enter Carmel at the age of fifteen. Louis reluctantly consented, loath to deny anything to his Little Queen. Uncle Guérin, however, was appalled and refused outright. When he had been persuaded, rather against his better judgment, there were still ecclesiastical superiors to be won round. Louis and Thérèse visited priests and bishops. Thérèse was invited to state her case and Louis nobly seconded her, but none of these good and prudent men would accede to Thérèse's tearful

pleas. Louis decided at this point to take Céline and Thérèse on the diocesan pilgrimage to Rome. It was a grand affair, patronized by the nobility and higher-ranking clergy. The party first visited Paris and made their way thence by easy stages to Italy, sightseeing enthusiastically en route. The pilgrims were to have an audience with Pope Leo XIII and Thérèse had conceived the audacious plan of asking the Pope's permission to enter Carmel early. She naïvely imagined that he would recognize the genuineness of her vocation and instantly grant her request. Instead he gently advised her to leave the matter to her superiors. Thérèse was heartbroken. Blinded by tears, she clung to the Pope's knees until removed bodily by a pair of Papal guards. Despite her disappointment, Thérèse enjoyed the sights of the return journey, Assisi, Florence, Pisa and Genoa. The party returned to France in December and on January 1st came the glad news that Thérèse was indeed to be admitted to Carmel, not immediately but at the end of Lent, on April 9th.

Thérèse spent only nine years in Carmel. During that time, her father suffered a series of strokes. His mind was so affected that he had to be confined in a mental home in Caen for a while, to the intense grief of all the family. Sadly, Louis, too, was occasionally lucid enough to realize his situation and to suffer the shame which was at

that time attached to any kind of mental disorder. He died at home in 1894 and Céline, who had nursed him devotedly, joined her sisters in Carmel in the following September. By that time, Thérèse had become assistant novice mistress and was delighted to be able to share with Céline her Little Way of humility, love and trust, a "new way to heaven" as she called it. Occasionally Céline herself became less than delighted — she was a headstrong young woman, used to managing her own life — and then she would tell Thérèse exactly what she thought of her. Between these rare outbursts of sisterly candor, Céline absorbed her youngest sister's teaching with enthusiasm. Later she was to be one of Thérèse's most ardent admirers.

During the winter of 1894-95, the Martin sisters were reminiscing at recreation about their old home. Marie suddenly suggested to Pauline, then Prioress, that Thérèse, who had taken a lively part in the conversation, should write down some of her childhood memories. Pauline hesitated but finally agreed and so *The Story of a Soul* was born. Written in odd moments in school exercise books, it tells Thérèse's story and expounds her Little Way. The main body of the manuscript took her a year to write, which brings us to January, 1896.

Thérèse had only a short time to live. In April, 1896, she began to spit blood and in due

course pulmonary tuberculosis was diagnosed. As this disease was almost invariably fatal at that time, there was little hope for her. Various painful remedies were tried — bleeding, needle therapy — but to no avail. At the same time, Thérèse suddenly lost her radiant assurance of heaven and was obliged to cling to God in almost total darkness. Her faith never deserted her but the radiance was gone forever; until her death the following year, she received only lightning flashes of divine consolation and, as she sadly remarks, these flashes made the surrounding night seem darker still. It was against this background of spiritual gloom and physical pain that she made her final journey to God. Already her sisters were beginning to guess at her holiness. They wrote down her conversations, sought her counsel, begged her to add explanatory chapters to her autobiography. She smilingly acquiesced. Calm, composed and remarkably cheerful, she awaited the death which seemed so reluctant to take her to God. Finally, on September 30th, 1897, she died, saying, "Oh, I love him — my God, I love you." She was twenty-four years of age.

After Thérèse's death comes the extraordinary story of her posthumous mission. She had promised to spend her heaven doing good on earth and she was true to her word. Instead of the customary death notice sent to other

Carmelite houses, it was decided to send copies of Thérèse's autobiography, which was published at the expense of Uncle Isidore. Soon the Lisieux Carmel was inundated by requests for further copies of the book. A second edition had to be made in 1899. This was followed by translations into both European and Oriental languages. The post brought requests for more details of Thérèse's life, for relics of the little nun whom some already considered a saint. The Martin sisters have often been accused of 'promoting' Thérèse. Worse, Thérèse has been accused of promoting herself. However, it seems that the Martin sisters, far from promoting Thérèse, were actually snowed under by requests about Thérèse. And Thérèse herself, in writing her story, had been seeking, not her own glory, but the glory of the God who had showered her with graces, inspiring her to share with others the discovery of her Little Way. "She who commends herself is not approved, but whom the Lord commends" (cf. 2 Corinthians 10:18). It was surely the Lord who commended Thérèse by working hundreds of miracles at her intercession. So it was that in 1909 the first steps were made towards Thérèse's canonization, which took place in 1925, just twenty-eight years after her death.

Thérèse will always be an enigma. She was so young, so very ordinary! During her short

time on earth, she uttered no epigrams, fell into no ecstasies, performed no miracles. Yet Pius XI described her as the star of his pontificate. What did this obscure young woman, from a French provincial town, have to offer to the Church and to the world? Perhaps her greatest gift to us could be expressed in a single word: color. We see a girl clad in the brown Carmelite habit; her blond curls, closely shorn, are hidden beneath the white coif — a model of piety, perhaps, hardly a riot of color. Yet Thérèse brought color to her world and ours — the bright colors of hope, enthusiasm and courage. She saw the Christian way as a glorious adventure, heaven as a country to be conquered, life as a battle to be won for God. She imbued the smallest details of life with the heartening color of significance. Nothing was too small, too unimportant to be offered to God, nothing was incapable of being transformed by the divine radiance. Thérèse brought — and still brings — color into millions of lives which would otherwise have been drab and cheerless. She told ordinary people that they, too, could become saints; and she told them that the way to God could be a way of happiness.

PART TWO

A SHORT-CUT TO HEAVEN

1

The Happiness of God

"The great and solid foundation of the spiritual
life is to give oneself to God . . . in such a way
that the good pleasure of God makes all our joy,
and his happiness, glory and being become our
sole good."

Jean-Pierre de Caussade[1]

Delight in the happiness of God.

Spiritual maxim, sixteenth century

THÉRÈSE OF LISIEUX had a
magnificent obsession: the happiness of God.
Four months before her death, she confided to
her sister Pauline, "I have formed such a lofty
idea of heaven that at times I wonder what God

will do at my death to surprise me. . . . So I'm already thinking that if I'm not surprised enough, I will pretend to be surprised just to please God. There isn't any danger I'll allow him to see my disappointment; I will be able to go about it in such a way that he won't notice anything. Besides, I'll contrive ways of being happy. To succeed in this, I have my little rubrics that you know about and that are infallible. Then, just to see God happy will be fully sufficient for my own happiness."[2]

The same theme recurs thoughout Thérèse's life. The small girl would ask her older sisters, and later her confessors, if God was happy about her. If he was happy, she would be utterly content. As she lay dying, she claimed that all her actions had been performed with a single object: to make God happy.

"Making God happy" was to become Thérèse's programme for holiness. It was the goal she set before the "multitude of little souls" whom she hoped to draw along her Little Way to heaven. These souls were not to scale the heights of spiritual endeavor for the Kingdom; instead they were to make God happy simply by loving him, and in so doing they were to find their own happiness.

This was hardly an original idea. To please God — which comes to the same thing as making him happy — has been the aim of all the saints

and to make God happy means to be happy one-self. So Saint Clare could describe the religious life as "the path of hapiness"[3] and Saint Bernard could say, "When God loves me, he desires nothing else than to be loved by me: he loves me in order that I may love him because he knows well that all who love him find in this very love their joy and happiness."[4] Julian of Norwich goes so far as to claim that "we are the happiness of the Holy Spirit"[5] and Blessed Elizabeth of the Trinity urges us "to love with God as a friend . . . that is the secret of happiness, the secret of the saints."[6] Thérèse's originality lies in her championship of happppiness, not as a mere by-product of holiness but as an aid to holiness. Certainly happiness was the atmosphere in which she herself moved towards God.

Most of us would agree that to make God happy, or to please him by doing his will, is an excellent ambition. Being happy oneself, is a different matter. It sounds slightly frivolous, even self-centered — not quite our idea of holiness! Yet Thérèse insists that to be happy is an important way of showing our love for God, for he loves happy souls, those who are perfectly attuned to him, content with all he wills or permits. The happy soul has faith in the loving providence of God, even in times of darkness and perplexity. Thérèse tells us that even when she

could not understand the why and the where-fore, she would smile, give thanks, look happy. The happy soul, according to Thérèse, tries to look at life from God's point of view; this is the opposite of self-centeredness. "It's quite bad enough for God," she says, "loving us as he does, to be obliged to leave us on earth to fulfil our time of trial, without our constantly telling him how miserable we are.[7] . . . When will you learn to hide your troubles from him or tell him gaily that you are happy to suffer for him?"[8]

Happiness, for Thérèse, is an expression of faith, trust and love. It is the eager response of the child of God to a loving Father. It is a sure sign that the soul is in harmony with God — which is one definition of holiness.

Once we begin to grasp Thérèse's inter-pretation of happiness, we may well wonder if she had the right word. Did she not mean 'joy'? Religiously speaking, joy is so much more re-spectable! No, Thérèse meant exactly what she said; she really was talking about happiness. For example, she made a clear distinction between "I suffer joyfully" and "I am happy to suffer." One could not always suffer joyfully but one could always be happy to suffer. Thérèse seems to have regarded happiness as a basic orientation of the soul; joy, on the other hand, was a grace which came and went.

Happiness was eminently suited to Thérèse's

spirituality. Hers was not a 'high road' to heaven but a 'low road,' a humble and imitable way. She wanted everything in her Little Way to be within the reach of little souls. Thérèse considered that joy — as a permanent state of soul — was beyond the reach of most people, including herself. It was all very well, she thought, for the great saints to rise above the clouds — that is, to manifest joy in times of trouble — the rest of us just had to put up with the wet weather! Joy was the habitual, rather dazzling state of the spiritual giant, whereas happiness was more suited to 'little souls.' "Let us remain far from all that dazzles," recommends Thérèse, "loving our littleness and content to have no joy."[9]

That word 'little,' so dear to Thérèse, has given rise to much misunderstanding. It is usually better tendered as 'ordinary.' Her 'little soul' is not a spiritual weakling, even less a lazy individual who wants to gain heaven without too much effort. No, it simply means an ordinary person who is daunted, as was Thérèse herself, by the endless complexity of traditional 'ways of perfection.' Thérèse offers her way of happiness as an alternative but far from soft option. She calls it a 'short-cut to heaven' but it is no easy way.

Most of us, if we are honest, will admit that we are ordinary souls, striving perhaps only intermittently after holiness; and all of us, deep

down, long to be happy. That we can combine happiness and holiness is good news indeed. We could do worse than to study Thérèse's rubrics.

2

Happiness Discovered

What is the end of man?
To know God.

What is his happiness?
The same.

Calvin, The Geneva Catechism.

THÉRÈSE was not born know-
ing her rubrics for happiness but she learned
them early in life. It was at the age of thirteen
that she underwent a decisive spiritual experience which she calls her 'complete conversion.'
From then on, she tells us, she was happy. What
an astonishing claim! To appreciate it, we need
to take another brief look at Thérèse early
years.

The small Thérèse was lively, intelligent
and marvelously obstinate. "She's such a tiny

scrap and so stubborn?" says Madame Martin but adds, "All the same, she has a heart of gold, she's very affectionate and absolutely straight-forward."[1] She was a much-loved child, the joy and delight of her parents.

"How happy I was at that age!" recalls Thérèse. "Everything on earth seemed to smile at me; my path was strewn with roses and my cheerful disposition also helped to make life pleasant. . . ."[2]

This first happiness was to cease abruptly on the death of Madame Martin when Thérèse was four-years old. Thérèse tells us that her cheerful character underwent a profound change. The vivacious and expansive child became quiet and hypersensitive; a look was enough to make her burst into tears. Things were to get worse before they got better for Thérèse. Ardent and impressionable, she experienced extremes of happiness and misery. Joy and sorrow chase each other across the pages of her autobiography.

There were the years of struggle with shyness. Thérèse could not bear the company of strangers and only recovered her gaiety in the family circle. There was the miserable experience of school, which brought her the unhappiest days of her life. There was the shock of her beloved sister Pauline's departure for Carmel, an event which seems to have precipitated

Thérèse's four-month bout of chorea. Then there was the joy of being healed by the smile of the Blessed Virgin — and the misery of feeling that no one quite understood. The Madonna, whose statue stood beside Thérèse's bed, had smiled at her and cured her. But had she? Thérèse began to doubt it all; perhaps she had invented not only the miracle but the illness as well. . . .

One of Thérèse's deepest joys was her First Communion yet she returned from the altar in tears. Perhaps she misses her dead mother or her Carmelite sister, mused the onlookers. Thérèse assures us, however, that her tears on that occasion were shed for pure joy. This joy was supplanted by a prolonged attack of scruples, with which Thérèse struggled in vain until she decided to enlist the help of her four dead brothers and sisters. "Being able to delve into the divine treasury," says Thérèse, "I thought they should be able to get me some peace!" They did. "Soon a delightful peace flowed into my soul and I understood that if I was loved on earth, I was loved in heaven too. . . ."[3] Those words sum up Thérèse's early story; she had discovered that she was loved on earth and in heaven. She had not, however, discovered happiness except intermittently. She was not happy with her tearful, hypersensitive self yet she was unable to regain the 'strength of soul' which had

made her such a robust and cheerful infant. She was full of good will but her extreme sensitivity made her, at her own admission, "quite unbearable." In the end, God took hold of Thérèse's good will and used it to effect her 'complete conversion.'

It happened in the early hours of Christmas Day, 1886. Monsieur Martin, Céline and Thérèse had just returned from Midnight Mass and Thérèse was looking forward to opening her presents, placed according to French custom in shoes in the chimney place. A big girl of thirteen was really too old for such things but Céline wanted to go on treating Thérèse like a baby because she was the youngest. As she was going upstairs to take off her hat, Thérèse overheard Monsieur Martin exclaiming irritably, "Thank goodness it's the last year of this!" Céline glanced at Thérèse, now on the verge of tears, and urged her not to go down straight away lest she be too upset. But Thérèse was a changed woman. Drying her eyes, she hurried downstairs to open her presents. So merry was she that Papa's good humor was soon restored and Céline could hardly believe her eyes.

"Suddenly," relates Thérèse, "my heart was filled with charity, making me forget myself in order to please others, and since that moment I have been happy. . . . God had to work a small miracle to make me grow up in a moment,"[4]

she adds. It certainly was a small miracle but it had far-reaching effects. It set Thérèse free from her excessive self-concern and hence from her unhappiness. It was conversion indeed.

As conversion is essentially a 'turning round' to face God, it seems strange that Thérèse should have used the word at all. Had she not face God from earliest youth? Yes, but she still lacked the complete conversion which consists in turning all desires Godward. Like most of us, she had retained, along with her desire to please God, a certain desire to please self. She had not really learned to say "THY will be done." As Simone Weil says, "We cannot prevent ourselves from desiring; we are made of desire; but the desire which nails us down to what is imaginary, temporal, selfish, can, if it pass into this petition (Thy will be done), become a lever which will tear us from the imaginary into the real and from time into eternity and will lift us right out of the prison of self."[5]

God offers to us, as he did to Thérèse, a way out of the prison of self; it is his own way of self-forgetfulness and self-emptying, his own way of happiness. He is the God who breathed his own life into Creation, who emptied himself at his Incarnation, who poured out his soul in the death of the Cross. In Olive Wyon's bold phrase, "The happiness of the Christian God consists in being a redeemer."[6] And our happiness is to

join, according to our vocation, in God's redemptive work.

Thérèse's vocation was to discover a Little Way to heaven and to draw others after her. It is a way made up for the most part of tiny steps, small events, minor sacrifices, yet it leads to God, to the "summit of the Mountain of Love." What more could we want?

Thérèse found various paths up the Mountain. We shall concentrate here on four of them: Realism, Humility, Suffering and Spiritual Childhood.

3

Realism

"Out of the strong came forth sweetness."
Judges 14:14

THE OPTIMIST, according to Chesterton, is a happy fool, whereas the pessimist is an unhappy one. Both, unfortunately, are fools. The realist, on the other hand, is no fool and can be a happy person.

If happy realism seems a contradiction in terms, it is probably because realism is so readily confused with the unhappy folly of pessimism. "To be a realist" too often means to see only the seamy side of life. Realism in the theatre, for example, conjures up images of kitchen sinks; realism in literature, the crude or problematical. This is a pity because it detracts from the basic

meaning of realism which is a true appreciation of reality with both its good and bad elements.

The saints should be in a good position to be realists because they are so close to God who is supreme Reality. Yet some of the saints did such very odd things; they sat on pillars, talked to birds and sang hymns on their own funeral pyres. Were they in touch with reality or just plain "touched"? The answer is that they were gloriously sane and marvelously realistic because they had discovered that God was the only reality that mattered. Their eccentricities bore happy witness to the centricity of God in their lives. They practiced asceticism, embraced creation and faced martyrdom because God was real and they wanted to please him. Not only did they seek to please God in everything, they also discerned his presence everywhere. Their realism enabled them to make spiritual capital of both joy and sorrow. Such a realist was Thérèse of Lisieux.

Yet sometimes it is difficult to see the real Thérèse, let alone Thérèse the realist. Already in 1932 Pius XI was complaining, "They have watered down the spirituality of Sister Thérèse. She is a virile soul, a great person."[1] He was writing in those distant days when it was a compliment for a man to call a woman "virile." But was he really referring to the Little Flower, with her roses, toys and small children? Hardly

strong-man stuff! The Pope was doubtless think-ing of another, often neglected side of Thérèse. One has to search for it. It is quite possible to read a dozen books on Thérèse without coming across something like this,

"I fling myself like a warrior into battle!"

Or this, more lyrical but no less military,

"I brave the guns with a smile
And in your arms, divine Spouse,
I shall die, singing on the battlefield,
My weapons in my hand. . . ."[2]

This and similar texts suggest that Thérèse was not the simpering infant of popular piety but one who realistically saw life for what it is, a battle.

Was Thérèse in fact a strong woman or was she, despite her heroic outbursts, merely a sentimental child? Was she a realist or a dreamer? To discover the truth, we must ex-amine the evidence. At first sight, this is some-what discouraging, at least for those who seek a robust Thérèse. The eyewitnesses, particularly her own sisters, seem determined to sell us a sentimental and unrealistic saint. Pauline, for example, testified at the Process of Beatifica-tion, "As long as I knew her, the only part of her

that touched the ground was the soles of her feet."[3] This suggests that Thérèse was in touch with reality, but only just! In fact, Thérèse was an unusually earthbound saint; she had no desire for visions and felt that it is impossible to see heaven and the angels as they really are. Instead, she was content to find God in the ordinary stuff of every day. Yet Pauline continued to present an anemic image of her sister, especially in her book *In the School of Saint Thérèse of Lisieux*, where Thérèse's doctrine takes the form of a dialogue between the Saint and the Little Soul. Pauline does not deviate from her sister's teaching; the content is pure Thérèse. The end product, however, could be described as "Thérèse purée," not an appetizing dish.

The public, too, contributed to the watered-down image. In a Church still tainted by Jansenism, Thérèse's teaching of love and trust was most welcome. Instead of making the then fashionable offering of herself to divine justice, Thérèse abandoned herself to God's merciful love. Her Little Way of love and confidence became popular — and then slightly facile. Thérèse seems to have foreseen this development and "explained with great vehemence," recounts Céline, 'that if the authentic spirit of childhood was based on surrender to and trust in God, it was based no less on humility and sacrifice. 'We

must,' she said, 'do everything in our power, give without counting the cost, practice virtue at every opportunity, deny ourselves constantly, prove our love by all kinds of attentions and marks of affection; in a word, do all the good deeds in our power for the love of God. But since this is very little, it is important to place all our trust in him . . . that is what the Little Way of Childhood is all about.' "[4]   Quite a program and not so little after all.

But the popularization continued, with the inevitable dilution of Thérèse's original message. There were the *poilus*, for example, the rough soldiers of the Great War who took the little Carmelite to their hearts. Not for them the virile Thérèse! Her war imagery would have lent scant comfort amid the horrors of the combat zone. The soldiers needed consolation and refreshment so they seized on Thérèse's flowers and birds and little children. A man can do with a few rose petals in the trenches.

When we turn from the eyewitnesses and the public to Thérèse herself, the picture is scarcely more encouraging. We are faced with her language, her thought forms, her style, much of which may justly be classed as sentimental. On the one hand we have the girl who braved priests and prelates in her fight to enter Carmel, one of the most austere monastic orders. On the other, we have the little nun whose talk is of flowers,

toys, birds and infants. We sense a certain strength in Thérèse, yet we are often repelled by her apparent sentimentality. Perhaps we need to distinguish here between sentimental form and sentimentality itself. So before we question Thérèse any further, we might usefully ask ourselves what sentimentality is and why we dislike it.

Sentimentality may be defined as indulgence in superficial emotion. Sentimental people savor emotion as a wine-taster savors wine, enjoying the bouquet, then spilling it out to pass on to another vintage. That is an admirable approach to wine but an unsatisfactory attitude to life. It is unsatisfactory because it is shallow and unreal. The joys and sorrows of real life are not meant to be sipped and then spat out; their purpose is to challenge and transform us. Joy should make us more loving and generous; sorrow, humbler and more compassionate. We do well to shun emotion-tasting.

Was Thérèse a mere emotion-taster or did she approach life at a deeper level? Why, if she was indeed a robust soul, did she indulge in the sweet imagery of childhood, especially as she had at her disposal a more vigorous variety?

That Thérèse was spiritually robust seems incontestable. She died in agony after a painful illness borne with amazing courage. Like Charles II, she was an "unconscionable time

a-dying" but managed to smile, laugh and make jokes until the end. Until her last few days, she continued to instruct and admonish her novices with affection and vigor. Until actually confined to bed, she never gave in to bodily weakness, bearing extreme cold, constant pain and fatigue without complaint. Last but not least of her trials was the thick spiritual darkness which shrouded her last eighteen months on earth. "There is no longer a veil between me and heaven," she writes "it is a wall which reaches right up to the sky. . . . When I sing of the happiness of heaven, I feel no joy. I am simple singing of what I WANT TO BELIEVE. . . ."5

As for childhood imagery, Thérèse doubtless used it because it was appropriate to her doctrine of spiritual childhood. Strong herself, she felt no particular need of strong imagery. Also, we need to bear in mind that Thérèse lived in a sentimental era. It was the age of Little Dorrit and Little Eva, of *Le Petit Chose* and *Le Petit Duc*. Strong Englishmen wept over Little Nell, strong Frenchmen over *La Petite Fadette*. It was an age where the child, often brutally treated in real life, was idolized in literature. It was a time when the message of spiritual childhood would find a ready audience — and probably be as much misunderstood as in our own more cynical day.

So when we consider Thérèse's sentimental imagery, a certain *Sitz im Leben* is desirable; also a degree of relaxation! We can relax; there is absolutely no need for us to *like* Thérèse's little birds and toys, not to mention her children with dirty pinafores. We merely need to situate them in her life-story.

One of Thérèse's best-known images is the little ball; this is not an expensive toy that a child hesitates to touch for fear of breaking it, but a cheap rubber ball to be played with or discarded or even ripped open to see what's inside. Thérèse did not just pen that image, she lived it. That was exactly how she felt at the height of her battle to enter Carmel, a toy discarded by the Christ Child. She felt rejected by God yet was prepared to endure rejection for love of him. He was free, she reasoned, to do what he liked with her, as a child is free to discard or play with a cheap toy. Thérèse is not reducing her relationship to God to nursery level but doing precisely the opposite. By consenting to be a "discarded toy," she is showing selflessness and endurance, scarcely nursery virtues. So it is with all Thérèse's images; the sweet exterior hides a profoundly demanding reality.

On another occasion, Thérèse uses a toy to illustrate, of all things, the action of the Holy Trinity. (Those who say Thérèse lacks originality had better think again!) The kaleidoscope,

she observes, makes beautiful patterns with odd scraps of material reflected in the mirrors. The bits and pieces are our poor human efforts, the mirrors the three divine Persons. Is this a sublime mystery brought down to the level of a plaything? Far from it. Thérèse is reminding us of the gracious juxtaposition of divine power and human frailty. Without God's transforming grace, we tend to be a bit scrappy!

It is because we are weak, says Thérèse, that God is so ready to pardon us. Yet in our self-importance we exaggerate the seriousness of our failings. Thérèse likens everyday faults to dirt on a child's pinafore; God can soon tidy us up again. It is a pity to take ourselves too seriously.

Thérèse's images can make us uncomfortable. We may like to think our discomfort is purely aesthetic, but sometimes we have to admit that what she says is too near the bone.

The struggling soul, Thérèse tells us, is like a small child trying to climb the stairs and yelling for help at every step. Unless God stoops down and lifts us up, we shall never be able to climb "the steep stairway of perfection."[6] Thérèse discovered this through personal experience and so shall we.

The more we study Thérèse's imagery, the more we find the solid substance beneath the sentimental forms. The honeyed pen is wielded by a warrior.

Some of Thérèse's most robust spirituality is expressed by flowers. At first her floral imagery seems ordinary enough. God has created as endless a variety of souls, she says, as he has flowers. The "great" souls are roses or lilies, while the "little" souls are violets or daisies. This is not just a pretty thought. Thérèse is pointing out that most of us are "common or garden"; we may want to be lilies but we are in fact daisies. Thérèse the realist urges us to become our true selves, genuine meadow flowers rather than lilies or roses *manqués* — "Perfection consists in doing his will, being what he wants us to be."[7]

Perhaps the most misunderstood Theresian image is the Little Flower itself. It gives the misleading impression of sweetness and fragility. In fact, Thérèse refers to herself as a "little flower" only rarely; she usually prefers the more prosaic "grain of sand" which is trodden underfoot and forgotten. She did not want to be known as *la Petite Fleur* after her death; it was her Anglo-Saxon admirers who translated and popularized the cognomen. The origins of the Little Flower image are far from sentimental. It was Monsieur Martin who first suggested it when he showed Thérèse "some little white flowers like miniature lilies; and taking one of them he gave it to me, explaining with what care God had created it and preserved it until that day. . . . In it, I saw the image of my

soul. . . ."[8] Louis Martin had just received his fourteen-year-old daughter's request to enter Carmel and he was heartbroken. He relinquished his "little flower," not in an excess of sweet emotion but in anguished resignation. Later he was to tell his friends, "Only God could demand such a sacrifice."[9]

In Carmel, Thérèse was to develop her own sacrifice flower-language. A "flower" was any small act of mortification such as not answering back, not complaining or showing annoyance, doing little acts of kindness without being thanked. As a child, Thérèse had counted such "sacrifices" on a chaplet specially designed for the purpose. Later she stopped her spiritual book-keeping for she felt that Jesus did not want her to count her sacrifices. Instead, she adopted the happy abandon of a small child throwing flowers in the Corpus Christi procession. The child, she says, "will throw flowers and sing. Sometimes it will have to pick roses among the thorns and the longer the thorns the sweeter will be its song. . . ."[10] Once again, Thérèse has managed to redeem a potentailly sentimental image. "Singing among the thorns" requires fortitude of a high order.

Thérèse did not confine herself to spiritual flowers. She and her novices would sometimes shower the crucifix in the Carmel garden with real rose petals. This was more than a pretty

gesture, as Pauline discovered when she asked the sick Thérèse to throw rose petals at the nuns gathered about her bed. The horrified invalid refused, explaining that she couldn't do that for human beings. It was for God alone that she threw her flowers. As she says in one of her poems,

> "Throwing flowers means offering you, as
>   firstfruits,
> The least sighs, the deepest woes,
> My joys and my sorrows, my little sacrifices,
> These are my flowers."[11]

Thérèse promised that after her death she would let fall a "shower of roses." Most people associate Thérèse's roses with bodily healings. However, she sometimes procures fortitude for her clients rather than actual relief. She is not in the celestial slot-machine business, as she warned her own sisters, saying, "Don't believe that when I'm in heaven I'll let ripe plums fall into your mouths. This isn't what I had, nor what I desired. You will perhaps have great trials, but I'll send you lights which will make you appreciate and love them."[12]   The real Thérèse is forever breaking through the sentimental expectations of her entourage.

Perhaps the most dramatic breakthrough is in the area of Theresian portraits. Once again, a

family member seems to have been bent on obscuring the real Thérèse. It was an odd business. Céline, who knew Thérèse intimately, took numerous photographs of her and described her as "severe," "intrepid" and even "virile" — this same Céline produced a whole series of anemic portraits of her sister. It is true that Céline was not aiming at a photographic likeness. As she so wisely points out, "Sheer mechanical processes of reproduction, showing only the plastic structure of her face, cannot capture her soul any more than they can capture refinement of manners or the perfume of a rose. What I have *always* tried to do is to capture and communicate that indefinable quality which shows the true picture of her soul beneath her features." Less true, perhaps, is Céline's claim that "the eye of the painter is not deceived, especially when it is the eye of a sister."[13] The true picture of Thérèse's soul should surely have included both her strength and her sweetness, yet Céline's paintings concentrate exclusively on the sweetness and the result is a curiously "filleted" Thérèse.

For example, an early "Céline" shows Thérèse as a young child with her mother. Zélie Martin's strong features have been softened; Thérèse regards her parent with piously upturned eyes. A photograph of Thérèse at three-and-a-half tells a very different story. A

rather cross little face stares at the camera; here is a child with a will of her own! And Zélie records, in a letter of the same period, "She is more intelligent than Céline but much less gentle and, above all, almost invincibly obstinate. . . ."[14] A later painting shows Thérèse on her First Communion day. A rather prim little face is dominated by huge, souled eyes. This is certainly not the Thérèse who wrote of that occasion, "It was a kiss of love . . . long since, Jesus and Thérèse had looked at and understood one another. . . . that day it was no longer a look but *union* . . . her joy was too great, too profound to be contained. . . ."[15] Those are the words of a passionate soul. The same passion can be glimpsed in another childhood photograph, this time of Thérèse as an eight-year-old. The eyes are a curious blend of serenity and zest, the mouth a straight line of determination. Here is an ardent soul, full of life, eager to give and receive love. "To love, to be loved . . . to make Love loved,"[16] that is Thérèse's ambition. Towards the end of her life, she began to see that the giving and receiving of love was to employ her eternally, so she began to think of all the good she would like to do after her death. Céline managed to sentimentalize even that energetic intention. Her well-known oval portrait bears Thérèse's words, "I want to spend my heaven doing good on earth," but there the authenticity

ends. A wishful Thérèse fixes us with melting gaze; the eyes are too large, the mouth too full, the chin rounded instead of square. That is not the face of the young woman who exclaimed, "If only you knew the projects I'll carry out, the things I shall do when I'm in heaven . . . I will begin my mission . . . I'll come down."[17]

The more we sift the evidence, the more we discover the real Thérèse, shrewd, courageous, strong. Less and less does she resemble the Céline portraits, the holy pictures, the popular concept of the Little Flower. All the same, it would be a mistake to conclude that Thérèse's sanctity lay in her strength. As she often repeated, her sanctity started and ended in weakness. A few weeks before her death, she exclaimed, "Oh, how happy I am to see myself imperfect and to have such need of God's mercy at the moment of my death!"[18]

Was Thérèse then a weakling after all? No, not in the sense of being feeble in character. She was a weakling in the sense that we are all weaklings, in that she was utterly dependent on God for strength. And she was wise enough to realize that she could not "do it alone"; she could not become holy by her own efforts. She had understood the literalness of Christ's words, "Without me you can do nothing."[19] She could have said with Saint Gregory the Great, "I do not stand on a summit of success, I struggle rather in

the toils of my incapacity."[20] Yet her incapacity was not pusillanimity. She went on to affirm with Saint Paul, "I can do all things through Christ who strengthens me."[21]

Thérèse herself understood the interplay between helplessness and holiness. She understood and rejoiced. Her admirers and detractors have often failed to understand, and so have missed the real Thérèse altogether. Folk have persisted in looking at either her strength or her weakness in isolation. So there was the fellow nun who wondered out loud why people said Sister Thérèse was a saint; she didn't seem anything out of the ordinary really. And there were others who were lost in admiration of Thérèse's virtues. Thérèse did her best to enlighten them but with scant success.

"You're so patient!" they cooed.

"It's not my patience!" retorted Thérèse.

"You're so abandoned to God's will!" they sighed.

"God placed me there," explained Thérèse.

"Say something edifying to the Doctor," urged Pauline.

"Ah, little Mother," protested Thérèse, "let Doctor de Cornière think what he wants. . ."

Could they not see that her strength came from God alone? But the compliments continued, becoming more and more fulsome. She was told:

"Souls who reach perfect love like you, see their own beauty."

"What beauty?" cried Thérèse, "I don't see my beauty at all; I see only the graces I've received from God. You always misunderstand me; you don't know then I'm only a little seedling, a little almond."[22]

But it was no use. One day perhaps they would understand. Meanwhile, Thérèse smiled at all the fuss and remarked, almost to herself, "Everyone can bend over the little flower, admire her, heap compliments on her. I don't know why but that wouldn't add one drop of false joy to the true joy she feels in her heart, seeing what she is in the eyes of God: a poor little nothing and no more."[23]

4

Humility

"The cohesion of the body lies in each
one's realizing his own gifts and also reverencing
that of others. Humility is not self-contempt or
cringing to others. . . . The sovereign Master and
Giver has given me my own life and my own gifts
and I am not to shame him by shrinking from
making the best of it."[1]

CHRIST SAID, "Learn of me for
I am meek and lowly of heart."[2]   Yet how few of
us really learn from him the lesson of humility!
We tend to find ourselves other models — like
Uriah Heep or Shylock or even Burns' field-
mouse. For we cling to the curious notion that
humility means grovelling when in fact it means
growing — in fertile humus. And, making a point
of despising ourselves, we forget that in God's
sight we are infinitely valuable.

The humble Christ never grovelled and although he was despised and rejected by others, he neither despised nor rejected himself. His humility was profound yet serene. He knew no vain-glory; instead he sought the glory of the Father and he understood — as we are so slow to understand — that the Father's glory is reflected in the faces of his children. That is the amazing truth: God wants to glorify us. He wants us to be fellow-heirs with Christ, partakers of the divine nature. He wants us to realize with Irenaeus that "that glory of God is a man fully alive."

Pride shrinks from being fully alive for a variety of reasons: fear of failure, self-preoccupation, the desire for independence. Humility, on the other hand, moves us steadily towards our full potential. As Lefèbvre points out, "We should try to be what God sees in us. That is humility."[3]   But even if we desire to be what God sees in us, most of us do not become humble overnight. Humility usually requires a long apprenticeship.

Some people, it is true, seem to be born humble. Saint Thomas Aquinas, for example, was as small in his own esteem as he was huge in intellect and physical bulk. Some acquire humility, like Saint Teresa of Avila who remarked wryly that shedding one's pride was like peeling onions; it came off layer by layer and it made you

cry. And some have humility thrust upon them, like Saint Paul who saw in the light of the Damascus road that all his prized accomplishments were "just dung".

Thérèse of Lisieux acquired humility. As she lay dying, she turned to her Prioress, Mother Marie de Gonzague, and begged her to present her quickly to the Blessed Virgin so that she would be prepared for death. The Prioress replied that Thérèse was already prepared, for she had always understood humility of heart.

Always? Not quite. Thérèse had to struggle with pride, especially in her early years. According to Céline, the infant Thérèse was proud and stubborn by nature and Thérèse herself tells us that she had plenty of self-love. As a very small child, she was offered a *sou* if she could kiss the floor. Although a *sou* was riches to her. Thérèse refused outright, revolted at the thought of lowering her two-year-old dignity.

The lively, demonstrative child turned into a timid, hypersensitive little girl. Precociously intelligent, the little girl shone at catechism. One day when the older children did not know the answer, the priest turned to Thérèse. In my *profound humility*," recounts Thérèse, "that was just what I was waiting for; rising confidently I gave the answer without a single mistake, to the amazement of all."[4] Monsignor Knox, in his translation of Thérèse's

autobiography, puts a puzzled footnote, "It looks as if the Saint was being ironical at her own expense. . . ."[5] Indeed she was. Thérèse had sometimes been a conceited small girl; as an adult, she was happy to admit that and laugh at herself. The humble do not take themselves too seriously.

Aged eleven, Thérèse tried to make friends with a girl at the Benedictine Abbey school but her overtures were spurned. She tells us that her love was not understood; she felt it but would not beg for a love which was refused her. It is humiliating to have one's affection repulsed; Thérèse evidently felt it keenly but like the Unjust Steward, she was too proud to beg. Thérèse also relates how she once started to weep to attract adult sympathy but received a reproof instead. "It cured me for life," she says, "of the desire to attract attention to myself; the only time I tried it, cost me too dear!"[6] That was a wise reaction but hardly a humble one; Thérèse was not going to risk such humiliation twice!

All this does not mean that the young Thérèse was a monster of pride, merely that she had not yet acquired humility. She struggled on, resolving at her First Communion that she would never be discouraged; she would try to humiliate her pride.

Fortunately, God usually humiliates our pride for us. He does this by bringing us to the

point where we are forced to acknowledge our helplessness. Only then can we fully understand Christ's words, "Without me you can do nothing."[7] We all want to do it ourselves, to become holy by our own efforts. It is only when we reach an *impasse* and realize that we *cannot do it*, that we become willing to let God do it. This is a moment of truth and therefore of humility, for humility requires us to stand before God in truth.

Thérèse came to her moment of truth at the time of her conversion. She had struggled long and unsuccessfully to master her hypersensitivity yet she could not rid herself of this unpleasant weakness. Then, she tells us, Jesus accomplished in an instant the work she had not been able to do in ten years. Thérèse finally realized that although she could not do it, God could — and that is humility.

Thérèse had stumbled across humility while seeking something different, self-control. This is always the way with humility; it must be approached indirectly. The direct approach of self-humiliation is unlikely to succeed because it begins and ends with self. Once we have "humiliated our pride," we naturally desire to observe the result and we become ensnared by self-regard, itself a form of pride. If, on the other hand, God humiliates us, we no longer wish to gaze at ourselves but at him, "Seeing yourself so

— 49 —

worthless," says Thérèse, "you wish no longer to look at yourself, you look only at the sole Beloved!"[8]

Thérèse had learned her most important lesson in humility — she could not do it but God could! Eagerly she set out to learn more. She needed her enthusiasm especially during her early days in Carmel where her "first steps met with more thorns than roses."[9] Looking back, she felt thankful for the "fortifying waters of humiliation,"[10] but at the time the going was rough. Again and again, she found she couldn't do it. She failed to please Mère Marie de Gonzague; she fell asleep over her prayers. When misjudged, she sometimes had to flee, knowing full well that she hadn't the virtue not to justify herself — and self-justification was frowned upon in Carmel. She wept copiously when Papa could not attend her veiling ceremony — "Jesus left me to my own resources and I soon showed how meager they were."[11]

Gradually it dawned on Thérèse that her weakness was not a passing phase but a permanent state. She had longed for years to scale the heights of Mount Carmel; now she found herself at the foot of the mountain and realized that she was too feeble to reach first camp. The holiness of the saints seemed to tower above her; she was a mere grain of sand beside such peaks of sanctity. She saw that she was too small to climb

the ladder of perfection. She was a 'little soul' who acknowledged, "It is impossible for me to grow, I have to put up with myself as I am, with all my imperfections."[12] In other words, she definitely *could not do it*. Thérèse was undismayed, however, at this rather melancholy realization. She simply went on to affirm that *God could do it*. She had understood that God sees our weakness, not as a stumbling-block but as a foundation stone. Did he not reassure the discouraged Saint Paul, "My strength is made perfect in weakness"?[13] He does not ask us to be strong ourselves, but to trust in his strength alone. Holiness, Thérèse concluded, was a disposition of the heart which made us humble and small in the arms of God, aware of our weakness but boldly confident in his fatherly goodness.

Humble and small on the one hand, confident and bold on the other; it was an unsual combination and not everyone liked it. The seventeen-year-old Thérèse shocked a Jesuit confessor by declaring that she wanted to love God as much as Saint Teresa. Told to curb her presumption, Thérèse argued that she was not being presumptuous; hadn't Our Lord commanded us to be perfect as our heavenly Father is perfect? The Jesuit was not to be persuaded; nor was Thérèse, who had lost none of her native obstinacy. She stuck to her guns, sure that aspirations to holiness were compatible with humility.

Evidently she explained her views more convincingly to another confessor, a Franciscan, who approved of her ideas and set her "full sail on the waters of confidence and trust."[14]

Gradually Thérèse discovered what humility is — and what it is not. Firstly, humility is standing before God in truth, acknowledging one's weakness yet relying on God's strength. Thérèse prayed, "I desire to be a saint but I am conscious of my weakness and I ask you, O my God, to be yourself my sanctity."[15] Secondly, humility means acknowledging and using all God's gifts and graces. "Do not believe," Thérèse writes to a missionary priest, "that it is humility that keeps me from realizing the good God's gifts, I know he has done great things in me."[16] Thirdly, humility is self-forgetfulness. Christians tend to indulge in what Coleridge calls the "luxury of self-dispraise." Yet all too often we disparage ourselves only in the hope that others will disagree with us! The truly humble forget themselves completely and wish others to forget them. The ideal, according to Thérèse, is to be as small and insignificant as a grain of sand which "desires nothing but to be FORGOTTEN . . . not contempt, not insults, such things would be too much glory for a grain of sand."[17] Thérèse is right; there is a certain glory in being noticed, even if the notice is unfavorable! Lastly, true humility is simple, like a small child who has not

yet learned the tricks of false humility, the down-cast eye, the diffident disclaimer. "I am too small to be vain," says Thérèse, "I am far too small to compose fine phrases to make you think how humble I am; I prefer simply to acknowledge that the Almighty has done great things in my soul."[18]   Again and again, Thérèse returns to the language of the *Magnificat*; the humble soul, like Mary, is a soul which praises God.

"As long as you're humble," says Thérèse, "you will be happy,"[19]   and to be humble, for Thérèse, is always to "remain little." "Remaining little," she explains, "is to recognize our nothingness, to expect everything from God . . . not to become discouraged over one's faults . . . and to be disquieted about nothing."[20]

At first, "nothingness" sounds a bit daunting. Are we not all trying, these days, to escape from nothingness by developing our personalities, filling our lives with meaning? We have a horror of being faceless non-entities, swallowed up by the crowd. And we are quite right to feel so, for Christianity does not invite us to such a dismal fate! When Thérèse says, "I am nothing," she means *nothing apart from God*. For the Chris-tian, "nothingness" is the logical outcome of creatureliness. As dependent creatures, we can do nothing without God; in him we can "do all things." Nothingness does not imply faceless-ness. As Saint Augustine assures us, although

without Christ we are nothing, in him we are Christ as well as ourselves. The saints were very much themselves yet they all confessed that they were nothing. Their nothingness was not the negative void which so alarms us but the happy dependence of the sons and daughters of God.

If Thérèse's "nothingness" requires explanation, so does her "everything." To "expect everything from God" is not Quietism; it does not mean letting the hands hang idle. It means relying on God rather than on our own efforts. But God requires our efforts; he sows the seeds of grace in our hearts but he expects us to nurture them. Thérèse is tireless in repeating that "We must . . . prove our love by all kinds of attentions and marks of affection, in a word, do all the good deeds in our power for the love of God. But since all this is really very little, it is important to place all our trust in him. . . ."[21]

Thérèse's next precept, not to worry too much about our faults, is even more surprising. Serious Christians tend to worry, and thereby become discouraged, about their faults. We make it a point of honor: the greater the worry, the greater the desire to please God. Thérèse, too, had started by worrying about her faults. Then a priest had astonished her by saying that her faults were not displeasing to God. She had never heard that before! The idea sank in and

became part of Thérèse's understanding of humility. If she was really nothing, then she must expect to commit faults; it was an inevitable consequence of her creatureliness. While pride is amazed to find itself faulty, humility takes it for granted. Thérèse makes this point in a letter to Céline, "We want never to fall? — what does it matter, my Jesus, if I fall at every instant, for thereby I see my weakness, and that for me is great gain. Thereby you see what I can do, and now you will be more moved to carry me in your arms. . . ."[22]

Finally, Thérèse advises us to be "disquieted about nothing." The humble heart is free from disquietude and fear whereas the proud heart is fearful and unquiet. The humble soul is happy to admit, "I cannot do it but God can," whereas the proud soul says, "I cannot do it but I'm going to make sure no one finds out!" None of us can "do it," that is, be exactly the people we would like to be. Pride is desperately afraid of being found inadequate to any of life's demands, so it takes refuge in various disguises. Afraid of being thought inferior, it boasts. Its fear of seeming dependent leads to arrogance. Fearful of being criticized, it condemns others. Afraid to be vulnerable, it becomes haughty or aloof. The proud soul is like a man in a fortress, anxiously patrolling the battlements, constantly afraid that his

frail ego will be attacked and exposed as worthless.

Thérèse shows us the way out of these miseries. If we put our trust in God's strength and mercy, we need have no fear. And as we lose our fears, we shall also lose our pride. Not all at once, but gradually shall we lose it; not by gritting our teeth and beating our breasts, nor by toiling up the heights of spiritual endeavor. "I can see clearly that you are mistaking the road," Thérèse told a discouraged novice, ". . . You want to climb up the mountain, whereas God wishes you to climb down. He is awaiting you below in the fruitful valley of humility."[23] God does not ask us to grovel in our nothingness but to grow to full stature in Christ. So the valley of humility is a happy place where we can relax, admitting our helplessness without God, yet rejoicing in the good he works in and through us.

Thérèse discovered all this and that is why, as she lay on her sickbed, she could say, "I saw through the window the setting sun that was casting its rays over nature, and the tops of the trees appeared to be golden. I said to myself: What a difference if one remains in the shadows or, on the contrary, if one exposes onself to the sun of love. Then we appear all golden. In reality, I am not this, and I would cease to be this immediately if I were to withdraw myself from Love."[24] Thérèse could not have done it — but God did.

5

Suffering

"Never was a skillful knight in a tournament so
gazed at as a man who suffers well is gazed at
by all the heavenly court. All the saints are on the
side of the suffering man; for, indeed, they have
all partaken of it before him and they call out to
him with one voice that it contains no poison,
but is a wholesome beverage."

Henry Suso[1]

"The happy ones of this world, I think, are those
with enough . . . self-forgetfulness to choose
the cross for their lot."

Blessed Elizabeth of the Trinity[2]

Once a visitor to the Holy
Land confessed, "I had never realized that the
Church of the Holy Sepulchre was the site of the

Resurrection!" That was slightly obtuse, perhaps, but it is a dullness many of us share. For we, too, often fail to see the link between death and resurrection. Rarely do we experience that mysterious blend of joy and sorrow, life and death which is at the heart of our faith.

The saints saw death and resurrection as two consecutive and constantly repeated acts in the drama of humanity's return to God and they behaved accordingly. The difference between most of us and the saints is that although we perceive this truth, we very often fail to behave accordingly. How many of us could imitate Peter and John, sore from a Roman flogging yet rejoicing to be counted worthy to suffer for Jesus? How many of us could sincerely share Paul's joy at being called upon to suffer for the Church?

Towards the end of her life, Thérèse declared that she had found happiness but only in suffering. This seems to be a slight exaggeration and is certainly more extreme than the testimony of the Apostles. Whereas they claimed to have found happiness in suffering for Christ, Thérèse says she found happiness nowhere else. Perhaps she is really trying to say that her *deepest* happiness was found in suffering for God. "Suffering joined to love," she says, "is the one thing I see as desirable in the valley of tears."[3] *Suffering joined to love*: here we find the key to understanding Thérèse's happiness in

the midst of sorrow and pain. Hers is no neurotic love of suffering for its own sake; she is happy to suffer only because suffering, for the Christian, is a means of union with God.

Happiness in suffering is one of the keynotes of Thérèse's Little Way. It is an attitude, she assures us, that is within the reach of ordinary souls. We need only faith and generosity. Also, for our encouragement, we should remember that Thérèse did not arrive at this attitude overnight. She admits that early in her spiritual journey she suffered sadly. It was only by degrees that she arrived at the point where she could say that she was truly *happy* to suffer.

The small Thérèse, like all normal human beings, shrank from suffering. As an infant, she howled and kicked when things went wrong; as a small child, she protested against pain as vociferously as most. Again like most children, she entered wholeheartedly into the joys of life. At this early stage, she could make a clear distinction between joy and sorrow. Joy was a loving family, flowers and feast days; sorrow was sums and scoldings and eating one's spinach. It was quite simple and there was no danger of confusing the two. Gradually, however, joy and sorrow became intertwined. This happens to all of us and the context is not necessarily religious. With Thérèse, brought up in an extremely devout home, it was only natural that the fusion of

joy and sorrow should acquire a religious perspective. So she learned that Christ had suffered death to bring us to the joy of heaven. To be happy with the good God, you had to die first — and not only did you have to die in the end, you were expected to die to yourself all along the way.

One hot day, Thérèse came running into the house demanding a glass of cold water. "What about denying yourself to help a soul in Purgatory?" suggested Pauline. Thérèse gasped and agreed. She was already used to making "sacrifices" for God, little acts of obedience, generosity and self-control. Like all Christian children, she was learning that the cross lay at the heart of her faith; the happiness of helping a soul was bought at the price of being thirsty like the good Jesus. The happiness of pleasing God was bought at the cost of self-denial.

This sort of thing is all very well at the nursery stage, except that it can make us into little martyrs or little prigs. Thérèse herself narrowly missed both fates but fortunately she did miss them. Her mature happiness in suffering is the genuine article. It is genuine in that it is firmly God-centered. Both prig and false martyrs suffer happily only if noticed and applauded by others; they require positive feedback to boost their egos. The genuine lover of God suffers for God alone, without thought of self.

It is only when it is selfless that suffering can become redemptive. Suffering is like a lever which propels us in one of two directions; either inwards to cling to our misery or outwards to cleave to God. Christ tells us that the single seed — which may be understood as the self-absorbed soul — remains alone; only when it falls into the ground and dies does it bear fruit. The seed is not thrown into the ground by an alien hand; it falls of its own accord — "*I* lay down my life," says Christ.[4]   So it is with the Christian sufferer; he or she falls willingly into the ground, confident of being raised again by the power of God. The Christian embraces suffering for God's sake and so embraces God himself and becomes caught up in the mighty current of his redemptive action.

Thérèse approached these truths with great simplicity. She never entangled herself in philosophical speculations about suffering. True, on her deathbed she exlaimed, "Never would I have believed it was possible to suffer so much! . . . I cannot explain this except by the ardent desires I have had to save souls."[5] Thérèse adhered simply to the teaching of the Church that it is a happy thing to unite one's sufferings to the redemptive sacrifice of Christ.

Now it is one thing to acknowledge the happiness of saving souls, quite another to be really happy when one suffers. Here it is useful to

distinguish, as Thérèse did, between joyful suffering and happy suffering.

To suffer joyfully, thought Thérèse, was to suffer "in the grand manner," not in the way of "little" or ordinary souls. Christ himself, Thérèse pointed out, sometimes suffered sorrowfully, so why should ordinary people have any higher ambition? When Thérèse talks of "happy" suffering, she is not speaking of the spiritual elation of joy but of a simple harmony with God's will. This may or may not be accompanied by feelings of happiness; the essential is to be able to say, "I *like* everything he does," To take an everyday illustration, a husband might say to his wife, "You go and have a rest. I'm quite happy to look after the children." Whether papa will have a joyful afternoon as a result of his kind offer, is doubtful, but the fact remains that he is happy to help his wife. The same basic attitude obtains in our acceptance of suffering for God's sake. We are usually happy with it rather than elated by it. In other words, we accept it peacefully. "Let us suffer in *peace*!" urges Thérèse. ". . . The word peace does not mean joy, at least not felt joy; to suffer in peace, it is enough to will whatever Jesus wills."[6]

Peace was Thérèse's passive response to suffering. She also made the active response of

gratitude, saying, "I thank you, O my God, for all the graces you have given me, especially for having let me pass through the crucible of suffering."[7] Suffering, for Thérèse, was not merely a trial to be undergone; it was a gift to be used gratefully for the extension of God's kingdom. Only suffering, says Thérèse, can give birth to souls. So she exhorts Céline not to waste the trials Jesus sends her, not to miss the opportunity of exploiting "this gold mine."[8]

A gift, a precious treasure, a gold mine — that is how Thérèse regarded suffering. Yet she never pretended that suffering was easy. In fact, she found she could only suffer a minute at a time, keeping her eyes firmly on the present moment, forgetting the past and taking care not to imagine the future. She elaborates this thought in a poem.

"If I think of the morrow, I fear my
    inconstancy,
I feel within myself both sadness and *ennui,*
O my God I am happy to suffer and be tried,
    But only for today!"[9]

Such sentiments show us a very human, very unpretentious Thérèse. All the same, the ideal of happy suffering may still seem beyond our reach. Thérèse comes to our aid with two

further guidelines, non-discrimination and personification.

Thérèse displayed a marked lack of discrimination in the area of suffering. For example, she spoke of the anguish of her father's mental illness as "a great suffering" and used the same phrase to describe her distress at breaking a pane of glass. We need not conclude that she was unable to distinguish trivial disturbance from serious pain. She simply saw no reason to do so. Suffering of any sort was grist to her mill. Christ underwent varying degrees of pain; there were the false accusations, the mockery, nails and scorching thirst, the crown of thorns, the desolation of apparent abandonment by the Father. Each type of suffering was needed to complete his Passion. So Thérèse simply accepted whatever sufferings came her way in the happy knowledge that all of them could be used redemptively. If suffering was precious, she reasoned, every particle was worth having.

Lastly, Thérèse personified suffering. It was never a mere phenomenon but always one of the faces of God. When she entered Carmel, she tells us that she threw herself lovingly into the arms of suffering. This was not a natural reaction for Thérèse any more than it is for the rest of us. It was a learned response arising out of faith and love. Thus suffering became for Thérèse — as it

can become for us — an encounter with the Person of Christ who calls us to resurrection by way of the Cross. Whenever Thérèse met with a cross, great or small, she rushed eagerly to meet it, as a woman flies to meet her lover. No wonder she was happy!

6

Spiritual Childhood

"Let us make our way through these low valleys of the humble little virtues; we shall see in them the roses amid the thorns, charity which shows its beauty among interior and exterior afflictions; the lilies of purity, the violets of mortification. . . . Above all I love these three little virtues, sweetness of heart, poverty of spirit and simplicity of life. . . . No, our arms are not yet long enough to reach the cedars of Lebanon; let us content ourselves with the hyssop of the valleys."

St. François de Sales [1]

"WHY DO YOU WANT your sister to be canonized?" they asked Céline.

"Only so that the Little Way of Spiritual Childhood she taught us may be made known."

There was consternation among the priestly examiners. Canon Dubosq, the Devil's Advocate, spoke up, "If you talk about a 'way', you'll ruin everything; you know very well that Mother Chapuis' cause was dropped because of that!"

"That's too bad," retorted Céline, "as I've sworn to tell the truth, I will witness to what I saw and heard, come what may!" There was even greater consternation when she had told her tale. "The gentlemen," recounts Céline, "had only set up the Tribunal out of *condescension*, and were sure there was nothing noteworthy in my testimony. . . . So I told them, 'I can't let people put Sister Thérèse of the Child Jesus into the same category as other saints; she practised only simple and hidden virtues and people had better get used to the idea.' "[2]

Céline was taking a risk when she insisted on the Way of Spiritual Childhood. God took that risk when he sent his Son as a child. Christ took it when he pronounced one of the hardest sayings of the Gospel, "Unless you repent and become like little children you will not enter the kingdom of heaven."[3] It was the risk of being completely misunderstood.

The Gospels do not record how the Apostles reacted to that saying. Saint John on the other hand does report Nicodemus' mixture of amazement and scorn as he asked, "How can a man be born again?" How can one become again a little

child? During the preliminary hearings of Thérèse's Cause, the learned judges, Nicodemus-like, thought the whole business beneath their dignity. "We no longer beatify kitchen brothers in the Congregation of Rites," sneered Monsignor de Teil, the Vice Postulator. Canon Dubosq even accused Céline of trying to bring Thérèse down to her level. Most of the Martin relatives rose in opposition. Canonize little Thérèse? Absurd! When the prospective saint's sister, Léonie, was told the news in her Visitation convent, she was working in the laundry. She paused long enough to remark, "Well, Thérèse was very sweet, but to make her a *saint*, that's going a bit too far!" and went on hanging up the washing. Mère Marie de Gonzague laughed aloud at the very idea. If they canonized Thérèse, they'd have to canonize half the convent. . . .

There *is* something absurd about a child bearing off the palm of sanctity. A child is so small, so limited. And when we question this particular child, we find at first no clue to hidden greatness. She even agrees with her critics by assuring us that she is not a saint but merely a very small soul whom the Lord has laden with graces. That smallness! We meet it at every turn. Even when Thérèse raises our hopes by declaring that the Lord has done great things for her, she goes on to say "and the greatest is to

have shown me my smallness and incapacity."[4] Thérèse repeats over and over again that she is small, that she is weak. Worse, she seems determined to remain within the limitations of childhood; she does not need to grow, she assures us, but to remain little and to become more and more so. No wonder the professional judges at the time, like many an amateur since, were perplexed, scornful and dismissive by turns. Yet Thérèse's Cause triumphed; soon the little child was taking the world by storm.

What did this child have to offer? Everyone soon found out; the authentic sanctity of the Gospel, the holiness which draws strength from the Cross. The simple souls who hailed Thérèse from the start, soon discovered that the Little Way was indeed a short-cut — up a mountain. It was simple and direct enough but uphill all the way and likely to bark one's shins. The sophisticated — the Popes, prelates and scholars who were later to be found among her clients — discovered the same truth: Thérèse's Little Way was *facile* in the French sense of being within everyone's reach but not facile in the English sense of an "easy way out." Behind the smiling Thérèse of the Child Jesus stood the heroic Thérèse of the Holy Face, the saint who "found heaven" in the veiled eyes of the Crucified. Everyone? Well, not quite everyone found the real Thérèse. There always were, and

probably always will be, her detractors who failed to see her strength and the adulators who saw nothing but her sweetness. Those who had eyes to see, soon realized that Thérèse was not offering to the world the Jesus of nursery piety; instead she was pointing to the Man of Sorrows.

Once our eyes have been opened, it is easy to discern the Cross in Thérèse's spirituality. Yet she does not insist on the Cross; it is almost as if she took it in her stride! Hastening eagerly towards God, she does not pause to lament over present suffering, still less to anticipate future ones. As she so wisely says, "We who run in the way of love shouldn't be thinking of sufferings that can take place in the future; it's a lack of confidence, it's like meddling in the work of creation."[5] What Thérèse does stop to consider are the attributes and attitudes of the little child. This has inclined people to think that Thérèse herself was a child who never grew up. Therefore, the argument goes, she has nothing to say to adults. Yet, had Thérèse in fact been nothing but a child, she would not have been able to write about spiritual childhood. The child, after all, is scarcely in a position to reflect on its condition; it merely lives in the manner of a child. Only when it is grown and has "put away childish things," is it capable of commenting on childhood.

Thérèse did not simply remain a child — a spiritual Peter Pan — but she *turned and became like a child*, a very different matter. She made a conscious return to the virtues of childhood — love, humility and trust — and she strove to develop these virtues at an adult level. The normal child loves its parents, trusts them completely and accepts its own limitations with simplicity. The normal adult has to learn to do all these things in relation of God. We have to learn to love and trust him as Father, we have to learn to accept our own frailty. Spiritual childhood presupposes a dialogue between adult and child, the child supplying the data (this is what it means to be a child) and the adult translating that data into action (this is how to live as a mature child of God). All the same, it is difficult for the casual reader to disentangle the "spiritual child" from the "mere child" in Thérèse's writings. Her language will always be a stumbling-block with its sentimental form, even the occasional snatches of babytalk. But those who take the trouble to penetrate this unpromising exterior will probably endorse Thérèse's own view of herself as a baby, but a very old one, a baby who knew a thing or two.

A real baby is helpless and frequently screams for attention. Even when it emerges from extreme infancy, it still lacks judgment,

responsibility and, to a great extent, originality. Thérèse's spiritual child is very different.

Thérèse, as the adored baby of the Martin family, was used to attention. She ran to Pauline with her childish woes, she confided her scruples to Marie. Yet she learned, early in life, to do without human consolation. When she was lonely at school, she would slip into the chapel to be with Christ, whom she regarded as her only friend. It is easy, one may think, to turn to God when human resources fail; anyone who does so will discover that it requires faith and fortitude. And Thérèse did not stop at that point; she went on, as a nun, to do without any consolation, human or divine. She refused to clamor for divine attention and comfort. As she says, there are many who serve Jesus in times of consolation, few who will allow him to sleep on the waves, few who will watch with him in the Garden. Thérèse was not the sort of child who cried for attention; nor was she lacking in judgment.

A small child lacks judgment; it has insufficient knowledge and experience to "take the better things and leave the worse ones."[6] Thérèse had no ambition to be such a child. She prayed rather that she might see the truth in all things. Her prayer seems to have been answered. "I would never have believed that such

good judgment was possible in a fifteen-year-old," marvelled Mère Marie de Gonzague.

Thérèse's good judgment was put to the test when she was made assistant novice mistress. In the first place, she had the good sense to realize that the task was beyond her. Many a girl in her early twenties, flattered by being given such responsibility, would have gone ahead blithely unaware of the pitfalls. Thérèse remarked soberly that doing good to others' souls without God's help was as impossible as making the sun shine at midnight. . . . Her solution to the problem was to throw herself trustingly into God's arms. However, she had no intention of leaving all the work to God! It was to gain wisdom, not shelter, that she sought God's embraces. His arms provided a vantage point from which she could plan her campaign against the faults and failings of the neophytes.

Sound judgment in moral theology was one of Thérèse's weapons in the fight. Despite her prim upbringing, she was able to reassure a troubled novice that even serious sins against purity were much less serious than the least sin of pride. God knows our frailty and understands our struggle with the sins of the flesh; pride, according to Thérèse, is much less excusable.

Thérèse had the gift of getting to the heart of the matter. She saw religious life as a search for truth on both the theological and personal

planes. So she was quick to expose any untruth in herself and others. True to the Gospel, she removed the beams from her own eyes first. For example, on the occasion of her delayed profession of religious vows, she was bitterly disappointed. She quickly saw, however, that her disappointment, far from proceeding from a desire to please God, actually sprang from a mixture of self-love and impatience. Had she not come to the monastery to do God's will? Well, then, she would wait as long as he wanted her to. She was equally clear-sighted about motives when a novice smugly announced that she had been overlooked in the distribution of dessert, thinking that a fine penance. "Go to the kitchen and ask for your dessert," said Thérèse. "Let that be your penance!"

Ceasless vigilance was Thérèse's program for her novices. She saw herself as a little dog guarding the sheep (and snapping at their heels occasionally). She was also a watchman in a high tower and could see the enemy from afar. "She never let us get away with a thing!" recalled Céline who spent her novitiate under Thérèse's zealous tutelage. Yet Thérèse's zeal was tempered by compassion; when she scolded her novices, she would sometimes weep with them. Always she would assure them that her rebukes had but one end in view, their perfection.

Thérèse's dream of perfection, both for herself and others, was a detailed dream; every little thing must be just right. This may lead us to question her good judgment. Had not the great Teresa taught that God was "not concerned with a heap of trifles"? Did not Thérèse herself insist that one should in no way constrict one's soul? Why then did she appear to revel in minutiae? Precisely because she recognized the truth expressed by Blake,

> "General Good is the plea of the scoundrel, hypocrite
>   and flatterer;
> For Art and Science cannot exist but in minutely
>   organized Particulars."[7]

To love God was both art and science to Thérèse; to love him was to be attentive to little things, "nothings that give Jesus more pleasure than the empire of the world, more even than martyrdom generously suffered. For example, a smile, a friendly word, when I would much prefer to say nothing at all or look bored. . . ."[8] These are the miniscule tiles which make up Thérèse's mosaic of holiness, the minute stitches which form her tapestry of perfection. We should not imagine, however, that Thérèse was interested in details except as means to an end. The end is

not the details themselves but the *tout ensemble*. As she practices each little virtue, she is like a yogi performing a complicated *asana*, the Sun Salutation, for example: stand, bend backwards then forwards, kneel, press upwards then downwards, bend low, rise again. Each of these movements is small and unspectacular in itself; performed in sequence, they make one glorious act of praise. Seen from this angle, Thérèse's preoccupation with detail makes excellent sense.

Clearly Thérèse's spiritual child has sound judgment. It is also responsible. A responsible child is one who assumes responsibility for the affairs within its scope, such as toys or lesson books. We do not except a child to be responsible for choosing its own school or earning its own living. Spiritual childhood, suggests Thérèse, is not a matter of being irresponsible but of seeing where one's true responsibilities lie. Admittedly, a cursory glance at Thérèse's thought does not convey an impression of responsibility. We find her declaring that she does not want to grow up, or recommending that we think of ourselves as very small souls, needing God's succor at every step. We hear her telling Céline that she is too small to understand what God is doing in her soul. All this is disconcerting until we realize that Thérèse is in fact saying something like this: we are mistaken — and spiritually

immature — if we think we can "do it alone" in the spiritual life. If we imagine we can outgrow our dependence on God, it shows merely that we have reached spiritual adolescenece, a time of rebellion and rejection of authority. If we think we can understand the mysterious workings of God in our souls, we are, to say the least, conceited. Thérèse eschews "responsibility" of that sort. On the other hand, she stress that we are answerable for the quality of our response to God. We must do all we possibly can to prove our love for him. That is where our true responsibility lies. Having acknowledged our dependence on God, we are to become energetic co-workers with him; that is the essence of Christian responsibility.

So Thérèse, the spiritual child, is a mature child, emotionally independent, sound in judgment, responsible. Is she also, as some have claimed, an original child? In one sense, of course, all children are original. Each is unique and unrepeatable. On the other hand, the child is unoriginal in the sense that it is to a large extent a reflection of its surroundings. After emerging from infant symbiosis, it still remains an imitative creature, learning reactions, speech and skills from its elders. Some have maintained that Thérèse was just such a child.

Thérèse herself claimed originality. She said she had found a completely new way to heaven.

She spoke of her "little doctrine" and her "mission" as if she were breaking new ground. Yet her teaching can be summed up like this: Christian perfection is attainable through childlike trust and surrender to God, who is above all a loving Father, ready to encourage our least efforts to please him, ready to pardon and succor his children, however feeble and frail. All this had been said before, with the eloquence of a Saint François de Sales, the polish of a Bossuet, the penetration of a de Caussade. All this had been lived before; have not all the saints insisted on humble dependence on God? Why then did Thérèse Martin and her admirers feel that she had discovered something new? If the story had already appeared in the more intellectual papers, why was everyone behaving as if little Thérèse had made a scoop? Thérèse's "scoop" was her particular presentation of holiness whereby she made it both accessible and attractive to little souls or ordinary people. We admire the great spiritual masters but we do not readily identify with them. If we imitate them, it is usually with diffidence and from afar. Thérèse, on the other hand, is a saint with whom we can identify. She practiced only simple virtues; we can do so too. What is more, she showed us that holiness is a happy state, a glad cooperation with the God who comes to us at every moment and in every detail of our lives. She demonstrated that "life

abundant" such as Christ promised is possible here and now, even in the dreary, commonplace or trivial moments which make up so large a part of any life. She reminded us that our vision of God need not be obscured by drabness, monotony or pain. Every event, however small and insignificant, can be a gateway to God's presence; at every moment we can pass beyond the narrow limits of ourselvs, into the happiness of God.

Endnotes

Chapter One: THE HAPPINESS OF GOD

1 *Self-Abandonment to Divine Providence* by Fr. J.P. de Caussade, S.J. (Burns, Oates & Washbourne Ltd., London,
   1933).
2 *St. Thérèse of Lisieux. Her Last Conversations* (ICS Publications. Institute of Carmelite Studies, Washington, D.C.,
   1977).
3 Letter of St. Clare to the Blessed Agnes of Prague.
4 St. Bernard *Sermons on the Canticle of Canticles* (Browne &
   Nolan Ltd., Dublin, 1920).
5 *Enfolded in Love*. Daily Readings with Julian of Norwich
   (Darton, Longman & Todd, London, 1980).
6 *The Spiritual Doctrine of Sister Elisabeth of the Trinity*, trans.
   M.M. Philipon, O.P. (Newman Press, Westminster, Mary-
   land, 1948).
7 *Soeur Marie de la Trinité, Une de Ste Thérèse* (Les Editions du
   Cerf, Paris, 1985). Translated into English by Susan Leslie.
8 *Saint Thérèse of Lisieux* (Burns, Oates & Washbourne Ltd.,
   London, 1926).

Chapter Two: HAPPINESS DISCOVERED

1 *Histoire d'Une Ame* (Les Editions de Cerf, Paris, 1983).
   Translation into English by Susan Leslie.
2 Ibid.
3 Ibid.

4 Ibid.

5 Simone Weil, *Waiting on God* (Routledge & Kegan Paul, London, 1951).

6 Olive Wyon, *Self Examination in the Light of the Beatitudes* (forward Movement Publications, Ohio).

Chapter Three: REALISM

1 Letter of Pius XI to the Bishop of Bayeux, 1932.

2 *Poésies*, trans. Susan Leslie (Les Editions du Cerf, 1979).

3 Process of Beatification. *St. Thérèse of Lisieux by Those Who Knew Her* (Veritas Publications, Dublin, 1975).

4 Ibid.

5 *Histoire d'une Ame.*

6 Ibid.

7 Ibid.

8 Ibid.

9 Ibid.

10 Ibid.

11 *Poésies.*

12 *St. Thérèse of Lisieux.* Her Last Conversations. (ICS Publications, Institute of Carmelite Studies, Washington, D.C., 1977).

13 Statement of February 11, 1950, by Céline, quoted by Pére François de Sainte-Marie, O.C.D., in *The Photograph Album of St. Thérèse of Lisieux* (Harvill Press, London, 1962).

14 *Histoire d'une Ame.*

15 Ibid.

16 *Last Conversations.*

17 Ibid.

18 Ibid.

19 John 15:5.

20 From the *Homilies of St. Gregory the Great on the book of Ezekiel*, trans. by Susan Leslie.

21 Philippians 4:13.

22 Thérèse's answers are taken from *Last Conversations*, the questions being supplied by the present author.

23 *Histoire d'une Ame.*

Chapter Four: HUMILITY

1 Charles Gore, *St. Paul's Epistle to the Romans* (John Murray, London, 1900).
2 Matthew 11:29.
3 Georges Lefèbre, *Simplicity, the Heart of Prayer* (Darton, Longman & Todd, London, 1975).
4 *Histoire d'une Ame.*
5 Knox, *Autobiography of a Saint* (Harvill Press, London, 1958).
6 *Histoire d'une Ame.*
7 John 15:5.
8 *The Collected Letters of St. Thérèse of Lisieux* (Sheed & Ward, London, 1949).
9 *Histoire d'une Ame.*
10 Ibid.
11 Ibid.
12 Ibid.
13 2 Corinthians 12:9.
14 *Histoire d'une Ame.*
15 Ibid.
16 *Collected Letters, op. cit.*
17 Ibid.
18 *Histoire d'une Ame.*
19 *Last Conversations, op. cit.*
20 Ibid.
21 Process of Beatification, *op. cit.*
22 *Collected Letters.*
23 *Last Conversations.*

Chapter Five: SUFFERING

1 Henry Suso, *The Little Book of Eternal Wisdom* (R & T. Washbourne, London, 1910).
2 *Blessed Elisabeth of the Trinity, op. cit.,* ch. 1.
3 *Collected Letters.*
4 John 10:15.
5 *Last Conversations.*

6 *Collected Letters.*
7 *Histoire d'une Ame.*
8 *Collected Letters.*
9 *Poésies.*

Chapter Six: SPIRITUAL CHILDHOOD

1 *The Spiritual Conferences, Book VI,* Library of St. François de Sales (Burns & Oates, London, 1883).
2 *Céline.* Stephane-Joseph Piat, O.F.M. (Office Central de Lisieux, 1964).
3 Matthew 18:3.
4 *Histoire d'une Ame.*
5 *Last Conversations.*
6 Hilaire Belloc, *Collected Verse* (Penguin Books Ltd., 1958).
7 *Poetry & Prose of William Blake* ('Jerusalem', Nonesuch Press, London, 1943).
8 *Collected Letters.*

Bibliography

Sources

Thérèse of Lisieux, *Autobiography of a Saint*, trans. Ronald Knox (Harvill Press, London, 1958).

The Collected Letters of St. Thérèse of Lisieux. (Sheed & Ward, London, 1949).

St. Thérèse of Lisieux, Her Last Conversations (ICS Publications. Institute of Carmelite Studies, Washington, D.C., 1977).

St. Thérèse of Lisieux (Burns Oates & Washbourne Ltd., London, 1926).

Process of Beatification, *St. Thérèse of Lisieux by Those Who Knew Her* (Veritas Publications, Dublin, 1975).

Biographies and Studies

John Beevers, *Storm of Glory* (Image Books, Doubleday, New York, 1955).

Bernard Bro. O.P., *The Little Way* (Darton, Longman & Todd, London, 1979).

Vernon Johnson, *Spiritual Childhood* (Sheed & Ward, London, 1953).

Ida Gorres, *The Hidden Face* (Burns & Oates, London, 1959).

Hans Urs Von Balthaser, *St. Thérèse of Lisieux* (Sheed & Ward, London, 1953).

Alba House Titles

François Jamart, O.C.D., *Complete Spiritual Doctrine of Saint Thérèse* (Alba House, New York, 1961).

Marie-Pascale Ducrocq, *Thérèse of Lisieux: A Vocation of Love* (Alba House, New York, 1982).

Joyce R. Emert, O.C.D.S., *Louis Martin: Father of a Saint* (Alba House, New York, 1983).

Chronology of Thérèse

1873- *2 January*: birth of Marie-Françoise-Thérèse Martin, the ninth and last child of Louis and Zélie Martin.

4 January: Thérèse is baptized, with her sister Marie as godmother.

March: sent to live with a "wet nurse" — Rose Taillé at Semallé.

1874 *April*: returns to her family and home.

1877 *28 August*: death of Thérèse's mother Zélie.

November: the Martin family goes to live at Lisieux.

1879 First Confession.

1881 Attends school at the Benedictine Abbey.

1882 Pauline enters Carmel.

1882- *December-May*: Thérèse suffers from
1883 violent attacks of chorea.

13 May: is cured by a vision of the Blessed Virgin.

8 May: First Communion of Thérèse and Pauline's religious profession.

14 June: Confirmation.

1886   Marie enters the Lisieux Carmel.

Thérèse leaves school, studies privately with Mme. Papinau.

25 December: has the religious experience she described as her "conversion".

March: Louis Martin suffers a first stroke.

May: Louis consents to Thérèse's entering the Carmel at Lisieux.

October: Thérèse and Louis visit the Bishop Bayeux seeking his approval for her to enter Carmel at fifteen.

November: Thérèse, Céline and Louis embark on a tour of Europe.

20 November: audience with the Pope in which Thérèse begs him to let her enter Carmel.

1888   *9 April*: Thérèse enters Carmel as a postulant.

1889   *10 January*:   take the "habit" of Carmel, and becomes a novice.

1890   *8 September*: Thérèse makes her life-commitment, "vows".

24 September: starts to wear the black veil of the professed nun and is called *"Soeur Thérèse de l'Infant Jésus et de la Sainte Face"*.

1893   Thérèse becomes assistant novice mistress.

1894   Writes the play *"Jeanne d'Arc"* and acts the title role. Has her throat cauterized for soreness and hoarseness.

Death of Louis Martin.

Ordered by Pauline — Mother Agnes — to write her childhood memories.

1895   Becomes the "spiritual sister" of a missionary and starts corresponding with him.

1896   *January*:   Thérèse hands over the finished manuscript of the "Story of a Soul" to Pauline.

April: suffers the first hemorrhage from her lungs.

Finishes the second part of her autobiography.

1897   *April*:   becomes very ill.

June: completes the third part of her autobiography.

30 July: Thérèse receives Extreme Unction.

19 August: last Communion of Thérèse.

30 September: death of Thérèse.

1899   *September*:   the Story of a Soul (*Histoire d'une Ame*) is published.

1909-   Formal proceedings towards Thérèse's
1923   canonization take place.

1923   *April*:   beatification of Thérèse.

1925   *May*:   canonization of Thérèse at St. Peter's Basilica in Rome.

D0880445